Genre Narrative Nonfiction

Essential Question
How can people help out their community?

W9-AXQ-673

by Madhula Chopra

CHAPTER 1

Moving to the City

It's moving day for the Sanchez family! They are moving from the country to the city. Their friends helped them pack their car. Now they come to say good-bye.

The Sanchez family chooses what to bring to their new home.

The kids wave to their friends. They are sad to leave their house. But they are excited about moving to the city.

The Sanchez family drives through the countryside. They pass farms and fields. Then the houses become closer together. There are more stores. The family stops for gas in a **suburb**, a town outside the city.

Back in the car, the kids check the **route** on the map. Soon they see the city **skyline** with tall buildings and a bridge. They are almost there!

Along the way, the Sanchez family travels on a highway.

CHAPTER 2

Getting Around the City

There are many people and lots of traffic in a city.

Every day, people like the Sanchez family move to cities. Many of them live in apartment buildings. Their new homes are smaller. Most people don't have a backyard or a car. They walk to many places. Some may take subways, buses, or taxis.

In cities,
many high-rise
apartments have
a doorman.

When people move into an apartment, the **manager** of the building welcomes them. He or she shows them around.

The Sanchez family now lives on the 16th floor. They can see a park and other tall buildings from their windows.

Some communities make sure they welcome all new people who move in.

The Pavi family has also just moved in. A neighbor shows Mrs. Pavi where to buy groceries. She walks with her to the post office and library. Mrs. Pavi finds a book she wants to borrow at the library.

In many cities, children can walk to school because they live nearby. Parents sometimes walk with them. A crossing guard helps the kids get to school safely.

Crossing guards wear brightly colored vests so drivers can see them easily.

Some adults cannot walk to work. They need to travel by subway. A subway worker gives them a map. He helps them find the best routes to get to their jobs.

CHAPTER 3

Having Fun in the City

Parks may have swings, trees, and even gardens.

The Trent family moved to the city last week. Billy likes his new school. He doesn't yet know where to play outside after school. The next day his new friend Jim takes him to a park. Jim's mom watches them. They have fun on the swings.

There are many fun activities for families to do in cities. They have many choices!

On the weekend, they can go to a park. They can get a booklet from a park **volunteer**. It lists things to do there. The kids can play games like soccer or kickball.

Athletic events are a fun way to meet other kids.

People can also visit museums.
A museum guide gives them a map.
They find their way to different
displays. They will see interesting
exhibits and visit the gift shop.

People in cities can visit museums to learn
about art, history, or even dinosaurs.

This block party is raising money for a Neighborhood Watch program.

Some city neighborhoods host block parties. Neighbors cook food outside. Delicious smells fill the air. Stereos and bands play music. People from other blocks nearby join the fun. Sometimes they collect money. They will use the money to make their block safer.

CHAPTER 4

Giving Back to the City

The Lee family has lived in their new city for several months. They are thankful for all the help they have been given. They decide it is time to give back.

Some races are many miles long and last for hours.

Mrs. Lee joins a running club. She runs races for different groups that help people. She asks people to pay her for the miles she runs. Then she **donates,** or gives, this money to the groups.

Community gardens may grow flowers, fruits, or vegetables.

Mr. Lee decides to volunteer his time in a park. He works in its gardens. He feels good about making the park beautiful.

The Lee kids, Mio and Chin, have a great idea! On Saturday mornings they volunteer in a library. They read books to younger children.

13

Let's meet one more family.
The Smith family moved to a city
today. Who do you think might help
this family? How will they help them?

**Neighbors can help the Smith family
carry boxes to their new apartment.**

Respond to Reading

Summarize

Use information to help you summarize *City Communities.*

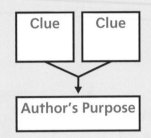

Clue   Clue

Author's Purpose

Text Evidence

1. How do you know *City Communities* is narrative nonfiction? Genre

2. Do you think the author is writing to inform, entertain, or persuade? Use selection details to support your answer. Author's Purpose

3. What is a synonym for *donates* on page 12? Synonyms

4. Write about the author's purpose on pages 12–13. Write About Reading

Compare Texts
Read to find out how animals in this
folktale get along in their community.

Magic Anansi

retold
Anansi
folktale

Anansi Spider has a friend, Leopard.
He also has a friend, Goat. Goat
has little kids. They all live in the
same neighborhood. They all live
in Leopard's house.

16

But one day, Leopard becomes angry. His friends have made his house messy. He growls, "Get out. I want this house to myself!" Leopard chases away his friends. They run through villages. They come to a river they can't cross.

Anansi comes up with a solution. He uses his magic powers to change Goat and her kids into stones. He throws the stones across the river. Then, he spins a long thread. He uses it to swing himself across the river. Now they are all far away from Leopard.

Leopard returns home. After a few days, he becomes lonely. He finds his friends. He insists that they come home.

"We're sorry, Leopard," they cry. "We promise we will keep your house clean!"
And they do.
Then they
live together
happily.

Make Connections

How do people in cities help each other? Essential Question

How do the characters in both stories help each other? Text to Text

Glossary

donates *(DOH-nayts)* gives or contributes *(page 12)*

manager *(MAN-uh-jur)* somebody in charge *(page 5)*

route *(REWT)* path or direction *(page 3)*

skyline *(SKIGH-lighn)* the place where sky and scenery meet *(page 3)*

suburb *(SUB-urb)* a town outside a city *(page 3)*

volunteer *(vol-uhn-TEER)* someone who offers free help *(page 9)*

Index

Focus on
Social Studies

Purpose To find out how people help out their community

What to Do

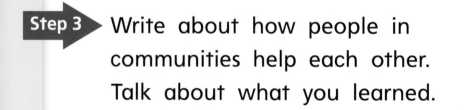

Step 1 Ask your friends how people help out in their communities. Talk about community workers and other people who help.

Step 2 Put your information in a chart like this one.

People	How They Help

Step 3 Write about how people in communities help each other. Talk about what you learned.

Thinkmark

The Topic

What is *City Communities* about?

Vocabulary

What new words did you learn in *City Communities*?
What helped you understand their meanings?

Conclusions

What conclusion can you draw about how people help in city communities?

Make Connections

What did you learn about cities from reading *City Communities*?
Would you like to live in a city? Why or why not?

Grade 2 • Unit 3 Week 3

www.mheonline.com

ISBN-13 978-0-02-119033-1
MHID 0-02-119033-X

Healthy Congregations

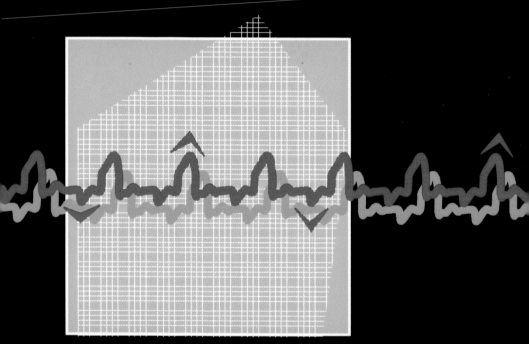

a systems approach

PETER L. STEINKE

an alban institute publication

What does it mean to be a healthy congregation? Beginning where he left off in *How Your Church Family Works*, Peter Steinke takes you and your church into a deeper exploration of the congregation as an emotional system. You will learn ten principles of health, how your congregation can adopt new and healthier ways of dealing with stress and anxiety, the role of spiritually and emotionally healthy leaders in influencing your church's emotional system, factors that could put your congregation at risk, and more. You will come away with a clearer understanding of your church's emotional system and a number of practical ways you can actively promote and encourage its health and emotional well-being.

"This book is about the stewardship of the congregation: how people care for, respond to, and manage their life together. It is about holding in trust the well-being of the congregation." With his opening sentence, Peter Steinke invites us to think deeply and reflect upon our congregations, our leaders, and ourselves. With an emphasis upon facilitating healthy people and congregations, compared to understanding pathology, Steinke promotes a focus that develops strength, options, and resources, In an increasingly stress-filled time, Peter has made a significant contribution to the ongoing process of understanding, supporting, and developing people in mission, congregational life, and leadership. I highly recommend it.

Paul A Parks, D.Min.
Executive Director
Director of Church Consultation
Samaritan Interfaith Counseling Center
Naperville, Illinois

Peter Steinke brings together psychological thought, material from the natural sciences, and theology in ways that make clear the incredible complexity of the congregational system, a system driven toward life and wholeness. This book provides a logical next step in systems thinking. Steinke tells us what potatoes, a small congregation, a forest, and a large congregation have in common. Each is a whole consisting of living, changing, interacting parts, organic units both susceptible to disease and able to use the disease to rebalance again toward wholeness. He presents a hope-filled scenario to a troubled church. Now, let us listen.

Conrad W. Weiser, Ph.D.
Psychologist and Pastor
Author: *Healers—Harmed and Harmful*